**Benjamin Bumpkin
and the Treasured Tree**

Also by Dr Colin Bonnington

The Grey Tale of Mrs Sciurus
Meles and the Ferocious Farmer

Benjamin Bumpkin and the Treasured Tree

by Dr Colin Bonnington

First published in 2018 by Dr Colin Bonnington

Illustrations copyright © Colin Bonnington
Front and back covers designed by Chris Freeman

ISBN 978-1-9999394-2-7

All rights reserved. No part of this book may be reproduced, stored in a retrieval system, or transmitted in any form, or by any means, electronic, mechanical, photocopying, recording or otherwise, without prior written permission from the publisher.

A catalogue record of this book is available from the British Library.

Any resemblance to persons fictional or real, living or dead, is purely coincidental.

For the awesome animals
and tremendous trees

Benjamin Bumpkin and the Treasured Tree

A Note on Trees: Pulverised to a Pulp

How many books like the one you're reading do you think you would get from an average-sized tree?

I know, I know what you're thinking; what size is 'an average-sized tree'? Well, say an 'average' tree is about 15-18 metres high, and say its trunk has a diameter of 45-50 centimetres.

I ask the question of course assuming that you are reading this as a paper book. You know, the old school type, and not on an electronic tablet or the like. If the latter, imagine an average-sized book and an average-sized tree.

So, how many do you think?

If I were to say ten books, would you be surprised? What about fifteen books? Twenty books? Twenty-five books? Thirty maybe?

Well, it's actually probably nearer thirty-five books, maybe a few more.

So, just imagine how many trees it would take to make all those books in the bookshop where you might have bought this book. That's not to mention the magazines, newspapers, greetings cards, pads of paper and the name tags pinned to the shirts of the shop staff. That would be a whole woodland maybe. And what about all those other bookshops and newsagents in your nearest town or city? Maybe two woodlands? And those bookshops across the country you live in … and across the world?

Then there's the shed load of other things that you make from trees. Sheds for a start! Wood for starting fires, wood for making doors, wood for furniture, wood for fences and gates, wood for xylophones, wood for smoking pipes, wood for toothpicks ... pencils ... chopsticks ... egg cups ... one of the three little pig's houses ... Captain Hook's leg.

You name it, wood can make it.

Actually, hold that thought; that might not be completely true. For a start, I can't imagine a wooden balloon or fire blanket, but you get my drift!

It's no surprise, then, that wood is one of the most important resources at our fingertips. Would you believe me if I told you that up to around twenty million trees are chopped down across the world every year? Loads eh?!

And, what if I were to tell you that trees have feelings just like you and I, so, every time a tree is chopped down to make any of these things, it feels pain like you would feel getting all your teeth pulled out at the dentist (without a jab), or getting the deadliest ever dead arm from the biggest, nastiest bully at school who is in a bad mood (without any padding) every minute for a full day. And that goes for every one of the twenty million trees going under the chop every year.

But I have a story which shows that some trees have had enough of this utter annihilation and are starting to fight back ...

Chapter 1
High and Mighty

The 'Popular Poplar' was a big tree, and I mean a really, really, REALLY big tree.

This is how big the Popular Poplar was:

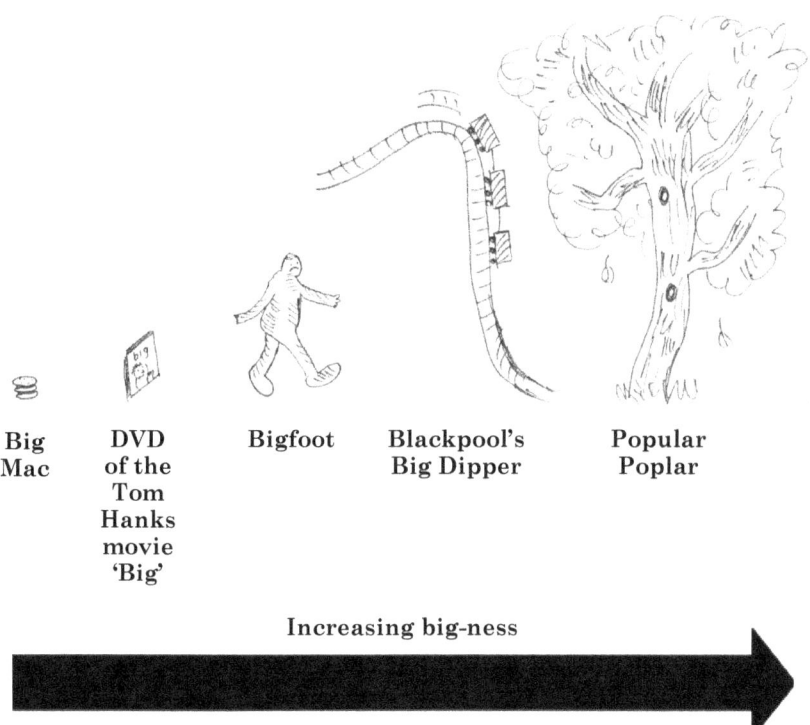

The Popular Poplar was a black poplar tree and reached to about thirty-five metres. It stood at the end of Jeffrey and Karen Bumpkin's back garden. There were other trees in the garden, but the poplar was by far the most impressive of them all.

The Popular Poplar was loved by all, from the bats and birds that lived in the large holes which peppered its trunks, to the young squirrels that had tremendous fun sliding down its huge, curved branches.

To Jeffrey and Karen, the Popular Poplar was stunning. They had lived in their country home for the last decade. Ten years ago, Jeffrey had been left Brockholes Manor, and its five football pitches' worth of grounds, by Sir Anthony Aardvark. Sir Anthony was patron of the charity which Jeffrey had founded, a charity which aimed to protect wildlife through community projects. Sir Anthony was so impressed by Jeffrey's good work and dedication that the house and grounds were left to him when poor Anthony snuffed it.

When Jeffrey and Karen had moved in the manor house was in desperate need of repairs, but the grounds were a hundred times worse. There are wildlife gardens, but the grounds of Brockholes Manor were more like a tangled, uninhabited jungle. Bramble had covered every inch of the gardens like an uncontrollable mould.

Jeffrey and Karen had decided that they would make the grounds open to the public, but first they had to clear the weeds and this would be no mean feat. They rounded up a few volunteers from the charity to help and, after two long weeks, the trees, lawns and immaculate shrubs could be seen again. The Popular Poplar was free from the bramble's clutches and people loved to come and see the magnificent specimen.

Things could not have been better for the Bumpkins and the Popular Poplar, that is, until tragedy struck the couple.

Chapter 2
Arrival and Departure

First, I'll give you the good news. Jeffrey and Karen married and, unsurprisingly, the Popular Poplar had a part to play on their wedding day. There were umpteen photographs of the happy newlyweds on their big day with the grand tree in shot. Like this one, with them hanging upside down from a huge branch by their legs!

Half a year later the Bumpkins were given the fantastic news that they were expecting a baby Bumpkin, a little boy. They had decided on a name well before he was born. He would be called Benjamin and the couple could not have been happier.

When the time came, an excited Jeffrey drove Karen to the local hospital. However, that excitement was soon to turn to shock and terror when Jeffrey was ushered out of the operating room to be told that his darling

Karen was experiencing some unexpected difficulties during the birth. Forty long minutes later a doctor took Jeffrey into a quiet room and gave him the devastating news that Karen had died during the birth, but little Benjamin was doing fine. Jeffrey's world had been turned upside down. This should have been a happy time, but he didn't feel happy.

Sometime later he walked into the room where Karen lay peacefully. As he approached her bedside he felt tears well up, and before long they were steadily trickling down his face. He held her hand tightly. He stood staring at her, willing her to wake up, but she didn't. He didn't even hear the door open behind him.

'Mr Bumpkin, would you like to meet your son?' came a hesitant voice. Jeffrey slowly turned around, to see a nurse. As she walked towards him, Jeffrey looked down into her arms. There, wrapped in a white blanket and sleeping peacefully, was baby Benjamin. Jeffrey burst into tears, this time with joy.

Chapter 3
Friends in High Places

The next few years weren't easy for Jeffrey; he was young Benjamin's dad and mum. But Jeffrey and little Benjamin had as strong a bond as any father and son could have.

Jeffrey would often take Benjamin around the grounds of Brockholes Manor and every time they would stop at the base of the Popular Poplar. Here they could stand for hours, with Jeffrey telling his son stories about the tree.

The trunk had gnarly bark, much of which was flaking, and the lines in the bark appeared to take the form of faces, like old, wizened men who would protect all that was good against evil. Sometimes, if Jeffrey looked intently enough, he would even see Karen's face appear in the bark, much like a mysterious image appearing, like the man's face in the moon. Perhaps Jeffrey only saw her face in the dark bark because he wanted to. See what you think. Perhaps you can find even more faces in the tree bark?

By the time Benjamin was three years old he would ask his father to tell him again the story about old Grey Beard who lived at the bottom of the tree. Jeffrey loved telling these stories, almost as much as Benjamin loved listening to them.

Now, not only did they love looking at the magnificent poplar, but Jeffrey also enjoyed climbing it. He had always been a keen climber and had all the ropes, pulleys and shoe spikes to grip onto the tremendous trunk and scale the giant. The view from the top was absolutely breath-taking, with woodland and the odd scattering of farmland sprawled out as far as the eye could see.

On some occasions, Jeffrey would strap young Benjamin onto his back and climb the tree to show his son the view. When at the top Benjamin would always say 'Wow!', but Jeffrey knew that wow was his young lad's new favourite word (if it was a word!), and he would say it at every opportunity, so he was never sure whether Benjamin actually meant wow or not.

On their way to the top Benjamin would pop his head into the holes in the large trunk to say hello to the local residents. In one of the holes lived a great spotted woodpecker. He was called Major Dendrocopos - 'Major' for short - and he was Jeffrey and Benjamin's favourite neighbour of all.

'Hello, Major!' Benjamin would call in. Jeffrey was always amazed that every time his young son did this the woodpecker would pop his head out of the hole, as

if to say hello. Of course, to Jeffrey the woodpecker was just looking at Benjamin and calling, but his son knew otherwise.

'Oh, hello, young Benjamin, my little star. How are you today, are you off far?' the bird would ask.

'I'm fine Major; we're off to the top of the tree. And how are you?' Benjamin would reply. Jeffrey would smile at his boy having an 'imaginary' conversation with the bird.

'I'm good my child, I like that you ask; today I have only one major task.'

'And what's that?'

'It's to eat as many beetles as my belly will hold, and perhaps a few more if I'm being bold!' he would say with a chuckle, rubbing his tummy.

'OK,' Benjamin would giggle. 'Enjoy your breakfast, Major. But don't eat too much!'

'Come back soon, my little chum, and hold on tight - don't fall onto your bum!'

'What's the Major having to eat today?' Jeffrey would ask as he smiled and turned his head around.

'Beetles.'

'What, again?' Jeffrey would laugh. 'He's going to turn into one if he doesn't watch out. Right, shall we keep going?'

'Yeah!' Benjamin would shout.

On reaching the top, Jeffrey would again be astonished by the view, and with every visit he would love the tree even more.

Little did Jeffrey know that, far down on the ground, three less-than-desirable characters also loved this tree, the Popular Poplar, but for a very different reason.

Chapter 4
Mr Grimm's Pies and Mr Grin's Puppets

Exhibit A is the first less-than-desirable character - meet Lofty Grimm. An unmistakable tall and lean eyesore, with his wild, unkempt and unwashed mop of greasy hair, a grimy bandana and sharp nose.

Believe it or not, Grimm was once a Michelin star chef in his restaurant, 'Grimm's Grillhouse'. I say a Michelin star, but actually Grimm just marked a star onto the restaurant sign with gold paint. Who would've thought getting a Michelin star could be so easy!

Grimm's Grillhouse worked on the concept of 'pick your own', much like when you pick your desired lobster in a fancy seafood restaurant. The customer would go into the courtyard at the back of his restaurant and pick the food they wanted. This included a few live cows, pigs and chickens.

'I'll have a bit of that,' the customer would say, pointing at the unfortunate pig.

'It is good for the customer to see where food comes from,' Grimm would jabber. Indeed, apparently the food came from a dark, dingy and damp courtyard.

Anyway, Grimm's Grillhouse had to be closed down after a series of complaints. These included...

A customer saying that they had a hare in their vegetarian stew (and that's not a spelling mistake, I do mean a full grown hare - fur, paws, big ears and all!)...

Grimm serving someone a shoe sole rather than a fishy one...

The chef being too literal with the ingredients of a RATatouille...

And to someone who asked what a fly was doing in their soup, Grimm simply answered, 'I think the backstroke!'

So, Grimm's Grillhouse became an empty house and Grimm fell out of work. He sold most of his kitchen equipment and just kept a cooker and a few pots, pans and dishes, just to keep him going.

By the time his money had dried up, Grimm had another money-making venture on the go - this time making and selling game pies. All animals were game to Grimm. Well, any animal that could be caught, trapped or snared, that is. He would cut the dead animal, whether it was a rabbit, a squirrel, a badger, a pigeon or an owl, along its belly and turn the carcass inside out so the meat, innards, bones and all plopped into a huge pot in one horrible mass. Grimm would then cook up the animal mix until it turned into a dark brown glop, add it into pie cases, and then ... voilà! (Don't worry that's the only French I'm going to use; partly because I don't know anymore!). Homemade game pies for sale - more like gruesome game pies, mind you!

But this was not the only 'talent' of Grimm's. You see, Grimm was a man who wanted to make money by any means he could. One day he thought to himself, 'What a waste jus' throwin' them animal skins away; I should use 'em.'

And use 'em' he did. Grimm discovered that the animal skins made perfect glove puppets, simply by inserting one of his hands into the animal where it had been cut. He could then move the head of the animal with his middle finger, the back legs with his thumb and pinkie, and front legs with his other two fingers.

Grimm soon became a part-time children's entertainer called Mr Grin. But, to entertain, he couldn't look anything like scary Grimm, so he made himself up like a crazy clown. He used spare blue food colouring to dye his hair, red food colouring to dye his lips, and a splash of flour to whiten his face.

As a clown, he also needed substantial shoes, so he used a couple of shoe boxes stuck together, with the lids stuck down, and a circle cut out of the top - one box for each foot.

To finish the look, Mr Grin wore his dirty apron and, inside the pocket of the apron, were always a handful of toads, which he would dunk in water and squeeze so that water would spray out of the poor creature's gob towards the delighted kids. Mr Grin was a clown on a budget!

He visited the nursery in a nearby village, where he gave puppet shows to Miss Key's class. From Octavius the owl to Percival the pigeon, the kids loved the puppet shows, and everyone was amazed at how realistic the animals looked.

So, whether it was Mr Grimm the gruesome game pie maker, or Mr Grin, the preposterous puppeteer, Grimm was a cruel, nasty man. And he would only get crueller and nastier after he had met the second instalment of displeasure. Meet Hefty Grievous.

Chapter 5
Grievous is Hardly a Cut Above the Rest!

Grievous liked to chop wood. In fact, Grievous liked to chop, chip, clip, cut and cube just about anything. Unfortunately, Grievous didn't always know exactly what he was chopping, chipping, clipping, cutting or cubing. You see, the dear fellow was a bit blind. He wore extra thick spectacles which sat on his round nose, on his round face, on top of his round body. Grievous wasn't a looker by any means. In fact, with his piggy eyes and wide mouth, he looked like he had fallen out of the ugly tree and hit every branch on the way down.

Surprisingly, Grievous was rather good at his job, and what he lacked in sight and looks he more than made up for in instinct.

He got to the final of a bush trimming contest, where each contestant had to cut ornamental sculptures into a row of bushes. Unfortunately, after successfully trimming a bush into the shape of the Leaning Tower of Pisa, and then the next into The Great Wall of China, and another into The Coliseum ...

... he accidentally trimmed a pensioner's perm into The Statue of Liberty, an Afro-Caribbean man's afro hairstyle into Sydney Opera House, and a young lad's candyfloss into The Houses of Parliament. Grievous was instantly disqualified.

He had once run his own legitimate forestry company which he named 'The Tree Fella'. He was paid by landowners who wanted trees removed and bushes sheered. He had his own green uniform and always wore a green baseball cap with 'Hefty Grievous' on it, presumably in case he forgot his name. But, after a while, Grievous got greedy and wanted more money, so he decided that he'd still chop wood and sell the timber, but this time without anyone's permission.

He would drive through the villages in his old, battered green van and stop at those houses with good-sized trees in their gardens. He would do his drivebys during the week, in the middle of the day when most people were out. He would simply knock on the door and, if someone did answer, he'd say, 'Sorry to bother you, but I was wondering if you need any trees cutting, or any other gardening work?' Normally the answer to this would be a resounding NO, and too many of these would mean a bad day for Grievous.

But, when no-one answered, that was when things got very interesting. He'd cut the trees down, chop them up into strips, fill his van up, and be home in time for tea. Grievous found that with his uniform on no-one ever asked any questions. It was almost too easy.

One time he even had one of the neighbours, a doddery old woman, come out and say, 'Arthur never mentioned before he went on holiday he wanted all his trees chopped down?'

To this Grievous replied, 'Oh really? It must've slipped his mind. He wanted them all cleared before he gets back on ...' Grievous paused and took out a diary from his shirt pocket.

'Friday,' the woman kindly interjected.

'Yes, Friday,' Grievous smiled. That would be plenty time to clear poor Arthur's garden of all his trees.

Other than the house visits, Grievous also found

visiting large country estates and plantations a good little earner. He didn't even have to knock on doors for these, and it was actually during one of these jobs that, by chance, Grievous met Grimm.

Grievous was in woodland in the grounds of a posh estate eyeing up an awesome ash tree, when suddenly he heard a rustle of leaves behind him. Grievous dived

for cover and looked around to see the other person also dive for cover, like a mirror image. As Grievous landed in a rhododendron bush, almost flattening it, a load of lifeless animals - squirrels, rabbits and birds - rained down on him.

'It must've been the gamekeeper,' he thought. But why was he trying to hide?

Grievous was stuck on his back like an oversized stranded sheep. He managed to pick himself up by grappling with the bush's branches, and he noticed the other figure was doing the same in the bush he had landed in.

'Are you the gamekeeper?' Grievous asked tentatively, brushing himself down.

'Erm ... yeah, gamekeeper, that's me guv...' Grimm coughed. 'Are you the forester?' he added, looking at the large axe in the round, bespectacled man's hand.

'Erm ... yeah, forester, that's me,' Grievous said, looking suspiciously at Grimm, who was looking back at him with the very same expression. They both smiled at one another.

'First time here too, right?' Specs asked. Sharp Nose nodded. The two men shook each other's hand. This was to be the start of the terrible trio, but for a trio you need three, and the third member was perhaps the nastiest and cruellest of the lot.

Chapter 6
As Bad as a Badger

Meet Tubby Grubb, and that angry mutt next to him is Grot.

Grubb was as bald as a coot, as small as a dabchick, and as bad as a badger. He walked with the grace of a Neanderthal man, with a hunched back and a non-existent neck. Grubb had harsh features and looked like a pint-sized Easter Island statue with clothes on. He always wore a frayed old brown bonnet to cover his billiard-ball noggin. Like Grimm, Grubb was in the pie-making industry, but, also like Grimm, pie-making wasn't his only money-making scheme.

Grubb started out as an animal collector and dealer who had travelled far and wide on the hunt for rare animals. He had gone to Russia and brought back a small bear which he'd knocked out with sleeping tablets and sold as an authentic Russian hat.

He'd brought a greater and lesser flamingo back from Africa and, having sellotaped both of their beaks shut and their legs together, had sold them as a pair of fetching gentleman's walking sticks.

He'd brought a family of rare snakes back from South America and sold them as differently-sized trouser belts, one for each of the family.

Two baby alligators he'd caught on a trip to the Everglades in North America had been made into a pair of shoes as a new must-have fashion accessory, where the wearer simply tied their feet onto the top of each mini alligator. The only problem was that you could only go the way the alligators wanted to go - and that was sometimes in different directions!

After visiting Australia, Grubb had brought back a kangaroo and, after tying its front paws together, had sold it as a rucksack which a child could hang around their shoulders. The kangaroo's pouch could hold a school pencil case and lunchbox, and the kangaroo (universally known to love a bit of boxing) could also act as an effective bodyguard against school bullies.

As well as these dodgy deals, Grubb also sold his most prized exotic animals – the ones he had smuggled out of their countries - as pets to shady private dealers. Grubb split the animals he had collected into a pet pile and a pie pile, where the most impressive specimens were grouped together to be sold as pets, whilst the less impressive ones were grouped together to be squished and minced to make the filling for his pies.

It was during his pie-making exploits that Grubb had met the serial animal obliterator, Grimm. The local village had run its annual village fête and had its usual food and drink awards. In the pie heat, Grubb and Grimm had finished joint first in the 'Gamiest and Gristliest Pie Award' category. The head judge had commented that it was amazing how both cooks got the pies as gamey and gristly. Simple, both men had thought. Be totally non-selective about the animal that goes in the pie, and even less selective about which part of the animal goes in!

Grubb and Grimm soon became friends. They say opposites attract, but not these two. The terrible trio of Grubb, Grimm and Grievous was now complete. The bad news for the Bumpkins was that the trio was not only complete, but also completely hell bent on getting their filthy mitts on Brockholes Manor, or, more specifically, the Popular Poplar.

Chapter 7
Roadkill Trumps

'That's the last of it!' Grievous said, throwing a piece of timber into the back of his battered green van; the van's under-inflated tyres strained under the weight.

'Right, let's get this wood dropped off at Shiver and Timbers. We're getting a good price for this lot from them,' Grubb called, slamming the van's back door.

'Sure thing!' Grievous shouted, walking around the van to the passenger side.

'Other side, again!' Grubb said. 'You sure you're OK driving?'

'Oh yeah, of course I am. I'm been driving for years and I've never been in an accident. Well, not recently anyway,' Grievous replied doing a 360° turn and heading to the driver's side. He jumped in, making the tyres strain even more, and turned the key in the ignition. The van's engine rattled and spluttered before miraculously exploding into life. Grimm, then Grot, and finally Grubb, piled into the van through the passenger's door. The four of them sat facing forwards, crushed together.

Grievous put his foot onto the accelerator and instantly the battered van went backwards and crashed into a wall.

'That'll be the reverse again you twit!' Grubb announced, looking at the dodgy driver and shaking his head.

There was a crunch of gears before Grievous answered, 'That's us now … at least I think so.' The dire driver closed his eyes and pushed his foot onto the pedal. This time the van pulled away at snail's pace, with the back bumper collapsed on one side and scraping the road.

'It's been a nice little earner 'round here,' Grubb said, composing himself and rubbing his stubby hands together.

'More trees than the landowners can keep an eye on,' Grievous added.

'And plenty of furries for me pies,' Grimm said with a toothy grin.

'Speaking of furries, who's up for roadkill trumps?' Grievous asked, turning to the others.

'Pigeon at ten o'clock!' he cried out instantly.

'Pigeon ya'say?' Grimm asked. 'Stop the van!' he cried, slamming his hands on the dashboard.

'Did you not see it? Are you blind, man?' Grievous asked, turning to Grimm and grinding the van to a halt. Grimm looked as the bespectacled man, thinking 'Am I blind?! Really?!'

'No, it's not that. I saw it aw'right. Just thinking it'd do in me next pie batch.'

Once the van had stopped, Grimm squeezed past Grot and Grubb. After a minute or so he came back holding the pulverised pigeon. 'It's a bit pongy, but nothing some seasoning won't sort out,' he said, climbing back into the van and tossing the bird into the back.

'Never mind your damn pigeon,' Grubb said looking dead ahead. 'Look at the size of that thing!'

There, over the wall to the side of the road, was the largest tree that Grubb, Grimm, Grot and Grievous (if he could see that far) had ever seen.

'Think there'd be a bit of cash to make off it, what with those other trees in there too!'

'And think of all the furries living in the garden as well,' Grimm added.

'Come on, let's get the wood in the back sold and we'll come back tomorrow for that beaut,' Grubb said, pointing to the tremendous tree.

'Does it look like anyone's home?' Grievous asked.

'Well, there's a car in the drive, so maybe,' Grubb replied, sitting up so he could see over the dashboard and down the driveway.

'In that case it may well be Mr Grimm that pays 'em a visit tomorrow then, rather than Mr Grin!' Grimm sneered, as suitably evil cackles filled the van.

Roadkill Trumps

Rules of Play

Now, if you haven't played roadkill trumps before, the rules are simple, and they sure pass the time of any journey whether it's from a car, during a bike ride or even a walk along a country road. But the game is particularly good played in a car (or an old clapped out van for that matter).

As many people can play as you want and the game is especially suitable for horrible people.

As soon as the first person sees a dead animal on or by the road, they shout what it is, and where it is in relation to the car.

For example, 'Rabbit at three o'clock!'

Usually it's obvious what the animal is, or rather was. At least one of the other participants must agree with the identification. If there is doubt over the type of animal, the driver may stop the car for all participants to check (assuming it's safe to do so). If the animal was wrongly identified the turn goes to the next person and the caller doesn't score.

Each animal has a score, ranging from common roadkill to rarer roadkill.

Low Score

Rabbit
Pheasant
Crow (including all black members of the crow family)
Magpie
Pigeon
Gull
All other birds, not stated
Fox
Hedgehog
Badger
Owl or hawk
Deer/ stoat/ weasel/ polecat
Pet (dog/cat)

High Score

The turn then goes to the next person going in a clockwise direction. That person then has ten minutes to see and shout out the next roadkill, and where it is, but the roadkill must be equal to (i.e. another of the same animal) or, ideally, better scoring than the previous one. For example, a gull would trump a magpie, and a badger would trump a gull, and so on.

If a roadkill isn't spotted within the ten-minute period then the person who called out the roadkill last scores 1.

The turn then goes to the next person in a clockwise direction, missing the person who didn't see a roadkill.

The game is played by some in a strategic way, in that even if you see a roadkill animal (for example, a rabbit) you may wish to wait until a better-scoring animal comes up, if the road appears to be particularly rich in terms of dead stuff. Bear in mind, however, that you only have ten minutes, otherwise you don't score and the turn goes to the next participant.

One other house rule is that even if the roadkill is in different pieces, it is still only one animal. So no second calling a badger's top half up the road, if its hind quarters have already been called before.

Enjoy and remember - you heard it here first!

Chapter 8
Miss Keys Strikes the Right Note

Jeffrey had no idea of the impending danger. He had arrived at the nursery to collect young Benjamin as normal and he stood in the corridor with his son outside Miss Keys' room.

'You're really enjoying your mornings here aren't you, Benjamin?' Miss Keys said smiling.

'Yeah! Especially Mr Grin!'

'Ha, yeah all the children love it when Mr Grin comes. He's got the most amazing animal glove puppets. They're so realistic, and he does the best voices for all the animals.'

'That's great, although he's always saying to me that the best thing about nursery is you, Miss Keys,' Jeffrey said, smiling and looking down at the blushing Benjamin.

'Oh, Mr Bumpkin, please call me Rachel.'

'And please call me Jeffrey,' he smiled back. There was a moment's pause.

Jeffrey cleared his throat. 'Right, anyway... Benjamin, will we get you back for some lunch? How does egg and chips sound?'

'Yeah!' Benjamin cried. 'See you tomorrow, Miss Keys,' he called, grabbing his dad's hand and pulling him towards the main door.

'Oh, Benjamin, remember tomorrow we have a trip

out to the zoo, and we'll need to leave at nine, so if you can get here ten minutes before that, that'd be great,' Miss Keys said, turning to Jeffrey.

'Don't worry, Rachel, I'll make sure he's here in plenty of time,' Jeffrey said with a smile, and he was pulled along by his son. Little did Jeffrey know that he wouldn't get Benjamin to the nursery the next day.

Chapter 9
Can't see the Wood for no Trees

The next morning, at first light, Jeffrey got out of bed and walked downstairs and into the kitchen. He unplugged the kettle and went across to the sink to fill it up. Before he turned on the tap he opened the window blind and looked out into the morning sun, squinting slightly. It was a beautiful morning; the sun had just peaked above the horizon. As he filled the kettle up he had a thought. 'That's strange, I can see the village church steeple now.'

Sure enough, over the top of the wall in the distance, the church steeple was as clear as day. As he turned the tap off he thought his neighbour, Mr Earl, must've cleared one or two trees. But it was when Jeffrey looked again, to the left and the right, that he suddenly realised that loads and loads of Mr Earl's trees had gone. In fact, all of his trees!

What was Mr Earl doing? Then he remembered that last time they met Mr Earl had told him he was going away for a couple of weeks to stay with relatives.

'I'm sure he said he's away now in fact? But he can't be?'

Maybe he should quickly pop over and find out what he was doing. Although Mr Earl was a quiet and private man, Jeffrey was pretty sure that he would have mentioned about clearing all the trees.

Jeffrey was just slipping into his shoes when there was a loud knock at the door. It made him jump, and so it should have.

Chapter 10
Unwanted Guests

Jeffrey walked to the front door and unlocked it. He could see through the frosted glass one shadowy figure standing on the path, almost filling up the whole of the pane of glass. He opened the door.

'Can I help you?' Standing in front of him was a round man with round glasses, wearing a green shirt and a cap with 'Hefty Grievous' on it. Jeffrey guessed he was called Hefty Grievous.

'Sorry to bother you, Sir, but I was wondering if you have trees needing cutting?' the man said in quite an odd accent. A bit posh but put on. Jeffrey suddenly thought about Mr Earl's trees, or lack of trees. Something didn't seem right.

'No, it's OK, thank you anyway. Bye,' he said, closing the door. Suddenly a hand slammed hard onto the door, stopping Jeffrey from shutting it.

'Excuse me?' Jeffrey said, looking at the man who had stepped up onto the doorstep and was now holding the door open.

'I'll ask you something else,' the man growled, this time with an accent not posh at all. 'Trick or treat?'

'Sorry, excuse me?' Jeffrey asked, his heart starting to race.

'Trick or treat? You know, as in, like, Halloween?'

Jeffrey was starting to panic from the man's sneer and his eyes flickering through his thick-lensed specs.

But, even in his panic, he still knew it was the middle of summer, and nowhere near Halloween. Jeffrey didn't have time to answer.

'In fact, let me answer for you!' the man yelled. 'This is definitely a trick!' And, with that, he stepped forward, pushing Jeffrey back and the door wide open.

At that point two other men - one short with a billiard-shaped head with a bonnet plonked on top and holding a lead with a snaring dog, and the other tall and thin, with a bandana on - stepped from either side of the doorway and scurried into the house.

'This is definitely a trick, but oh what a treat!' Billiard Head sneered, rubbing his little hands together.

Chapter 11
Under Lock and Key

Jeffrey was bundled to the hall floor.

'Right, you stay there!' Grubb shouted. 'Grimm, go check the house for others'. The bandana disappeared through to the sitting room.

'Benjamin, look out!' Jeffrey screamed instinctively.

'Oh well, I'm guessing there's one other anyway!' Grubb laughed.

'If you touch him!' Jeffrey shouted, starting to get to his feet.

'Sit down, champ!' Grievous shouted, pushing Jeffrey back down. Although Jeffrey was about the same height as Grievous, he was about half his width, so the round brute definitely had the physical advantage. The mutt stood by Grievous and snarled at Jeffrey, keeping a keen eye on him.

'No one 'ere!' Grimm said, returning into the hall.

'Get up the stairs!' Grubb yelled pointing, 'And look sharp!' Quickly, scaling two steps at a time, Grimm charged upstairs.

'You leave him alone!' Jeffrey called out.

'Or what?' Grievous asked, moving his weight from foot to foot. 'We're dead scared of you - NOT!'

There was banging and clanging from upstairs. With every noise, Jeffrey flinched and started to stand up again.

'Ah-ah! Sit down!' Grievous ordered, pushing Jeffrey down.

After a minute or so, but which seemed like an eternity to Jeffrey, Grimm appeared at the top of the stairs with Benjamin under his arm.

'We've got a wriggler 'ere!' he shouted, chuckling and walking slowly down the stairs.

'Get off me!' Benjamin cried, trying to kick out at Grimm. He was roughly slapped down beside his dad and Jeffrey quickly put his arms around his son.

'Thank God. It's OK. We're OK.'

'Right, we need to lock this pair away somewhere,' Grubb said, scurrying through the hall. He looked into the kitchen, and then out of the window into the garden. There, standing proud in the light of the morning sunshine, was the poplar - the top prize. Grubb smiled and then looked around the grounds - that's when he noticed a metal cage. Perhaps a rabbit hatch or chicken coop. 'Just the place for these two vermin.'

Chapter 12
Cooped up

The two rabbits in the hutch were unduly dispatched.

'Good for me pies, these,' Grimm said, carrying both rabbits by their ears into the kitchen.

'Not Carrot and Clover!' Benjamin cried, as he watched his beloved pets getting carried away. Jeffrey comforted his young son and put an arm around his shoulders.

'It's OK, they won't hurt us.'

Benjamin was still sobbing as they were locked in the hutch. Jeffrey tried to resist at first, but it was no good. It would be best just to let them take what they wanted. Besides, the main thing was to protect Benjamin, and he was now safely in his arms, both of them cooped up in the hutch.

'Right, boys, we've got work to do!' Grubb shouted, as he turned the padlock on the hutch door.

For the next few hours Jeffrey and Benjamin watched as Grimm attached long strips of double-sided sticky tape across the garden from fence post to fence post. He then appeared to remove all the panes of glass from the windows of Jeffrey and Benjamin's home.

'What on earth is he doing?' Jeffrey said under his breath.

Grimm brought all the panes of glass out and fixed them vertically into the ground, dotted around. Next, he set a whole host of different traps, large and small,

scattered across the garden.

'Just the job,' Grimm said, looking around at his handiwork.

Meanwhile, Grievous had set about the smaller trees in the garden. He had already chopped down two medium-sized alder trees, which he had cut up into strips for the van. He then turned to a wooden telegraph pole and started to chop at its base, before Grubb called over, 'Get better specs, you blind sod! Stick to the bloomin' trees!'

'Oh, right,' Grievous replied, looking up at the electrical cables extending out from the pole. He took off his specs and gave them a wipe with his shirt, pretending it was because his lenses were dirty that he couldn't see properly, rather than it being his rotten eyesight.

Next he moved onto a large oak.

'There's a furry in this one!' he called out.

Grievous couldn't see for toffee, but he had a sense of smell better than any sniffer dog. He could sniff an animal out at any pace, like a shark sensing a drop of blood in an ocean from miles away.

'In fact...' he shouted sniffing the air, his nose wriggling and twitching madly, 'There's one, two, three, four, five, six, seven, eight, nine, ten ... no, wait ... eleven furries in this one!'

'Fantastic!' Grubb yelled, scurrying across to the tree feller. 'Grimm, over here. We've got a few more tasties for your pies! And grab a couple of those nets will you?'

Grubb and Grimm armed themselves with a net each and positioned themselves about fifteen metres from where Grievous stood by the base of the oak tree.

'Right, Grievous, get chopping!' Grubb yelled, sticking his thumb up. The ferocious forester started to hack away at the trunk of the oak. Before long, the tree started to sway slightly.

'You two ready?' shouted Grievous, as he cut a triangle shape out the base of the trunk to direct the fall.

'Go for it!'

After another couple of hacks the tree fell. As it crashed onto the ground, bats started to fly out of a large hole. Frantically, Grubb and Grimm swiped the air with their nets, catching each and every bat that flew out.

After a couple of minutes Grimm yelled, 'Bats bring a real depth of flavour to the pie, they do!' He then transferred the bats from the nets into a large sack. 'Now it's time for these bats to meet my bat!' he said with a grin, as he looked across at his wooden bat which was propped up by the back door.

Suddenly there was a bang. 'Sounds as though I've had me first big hit as well!' he laughed, walking over to the panes of glass, one of which now had a dazzled songbird on the ground beside it.

'I dunno about four and twenty blackbirds, but that's one blackbird to bake in a pie anyway!' he chuckled, grabbing the bird and tossing it into the sack of bats.

Jeffrey and Benjamin watched for the next few hours as the garden of Brockholes Manor was cleared of all life. Grievous was felling trees left, right and centre, and Grimm and Grubb, and even Grot, were running around frantically grabbing stricken animals which had either smashed into the glass panes, got stuck on the sticky tape or got caught in one of the many traps. The terrible trio and the mutt would have the place stripped by night fall.

Grubb had even made signs, one saying PIE PILE (or 'PIE PiULL' if your spelling was as bad as Grubbs) and the other PET PILE, where the animals were put depending on whether they were fit for selling as a pet or for pie filling.

So far all the animals had been thrown into the pie pile so there was to be plenty of filling to make Grimm's disgusting dinner and, speaking of disgusting, it was then that Jeffrey caught a whiff of something!

Chapter 13
The Unlikely Uncles

The smell was truly disgusting, and it was coming from their kitchen.

'First batch of pies almost ready!' Grimm shouted, poking his head out the back door. Grubb and Grievous were kneeling in the garden, building a kennel for Grot with some of the spare wood. They had piles and piles of timber dotted all over the garden. Jeffrey wondered how long they were thinking of staying. He looked down at his watch; it was almost five o'clock.

'Don't worry, you'll get one of the pies as well for your dinner. You won't go without,' Grubb called, looking across.

'Oh great!' Jeffrey called back sarcastically. He looked down at Benjamin who grimaced and added, 'I'm not hungry'.

Grubb took a step back. 'There, that's the kennel finished. Grot, what do you think?'

The horrid hound waddled up to the kennel, shrugged and disappeared inside.

'Take it you like it then?!'

Just then there was a knock from somewhere. It took Jeffrey a few minutes to realise it was their front door.

'What do we do?' a worried Grimm called to Grubb from the kitchen.

'Just pretend no-one's in and leave it'.

After a few moments of silence the doorbell rang, followed by several more knocks.

'Just go away,' Grubb mouthed to Grimm. 'Right, go check who it is, but don't answer it yet, and make sure they don't see you.'

'Righto ... watch me pies, will you?'

Grimm darted through into the hall and dived into the sitting room, where he ducked underneath the window. He peered up slowly and peeked out the window, where he was met with the familiar face of Miss Keys.

'Mr Grin, is that you?' she asked, squinting and looking through the window.

'Please, Grimm,' he said, standing up. 'Just give me a sec.' And without thinking he went through to the hall and opened up the front door. 'Fancy meeting you 'ere!' he said.

'Yes indeed,' Miss Keys answered, hesitating slightly. 'I was actually looking for Benjamin's dad, Jeffrey. Jeffrey Bumpkin'.

Grimm had a think for a moment. He had wondered whether he had seen that kid before. Grimm wasn't one for remembering faces, especially of kids, who he despised. The Mr Grin act was definitely for the money, not for the children.

'Ehm, I'm Benjamin's grandad ...' he spat out. 'Sorry, I mean brother ... what am I sayin'?' He chuckled nervously, before finally settling on, ' 'Is uncle'.

'Oh, really?' Miss Keys said, looking suspiciously at Grimm. 'Well, is he in? Because I just wanted to make sure he was OK as he missed the zoo trip today.'

'In? Oh, yeah, he is. He wasn't feelin' the best today,' Grimm lied. 'Anyway,' he said, putting his hand on the door handle, 'best be off...'

'Who was that?' Grubb asked, walking through into the hall. 'Oh.' He stopped in his tracks and looked at Miss Keys, then at Grimm. 'You never said you were going to answer it,' he said though gritted teeth.

Miss Keys looked at Grimm, and then at Grubb. Something, in fact everything, didn't feel right.

'I'm Miss Keys, Benjamin's nursery teacher,' she said to Grubb. There was a pause.

'Ehm, well I'm his ... uncle,' Grubb said.

'Oh, another uncle?! How lovely,' Miss Keys said hesitantly, thinking that the two men in front of her didn't look anything alike.

Grubb appeared to realise this from Miss Keys' look and added, 'Not blood uncles, though!'

'Right ... could I see Benjamin, if it's not too much trouble?' Miss Keys was desperate to make sure Benjamin was OK, and Jeffrey for that matter. Yesterday Jeffrey hadn't said anything about Benjamin's uncles looking after him, and he'd said he would be coming to the zoo trip.

'Ehm, I don't see why not,' Grimm said hesitantly.

He turned to Grubb, who returned a 'Why'd you say that?!' glare.

'I'll go get 'im,' Grimm said with a gulp, and he backed

away and headed down the hall. Grubb forced a smile and looked at Miss Keys, but couldn't look her in the eye.

At the rabbit hutch Grimm stopped and crouched down outside the door. 'Oi, little man. Come 'ere!'

'What's happening?' Jeffrey asked, holding Benjamin firm.

'We've got Miss Keys at the door, wonderin' if he's alright. So he needs to come with me and say that he's dandy ... oh, and I'm yer uncle, right?' Grimm said turning to Benjamin, who looked at his dad.

Jeffrey wondered whether to shout to Rachel and warn her, but he could be putting everyone at risk so he thought better of it.

'Yeah, you go, Benjamin,' Jeffrey said and he gave his son's arm a reassuring squeeze.

'OK,' Benjamin said. He scooped some of the hard, round rabbit droppings off the hutch floor and put them in his pocket without Grimm noticing.

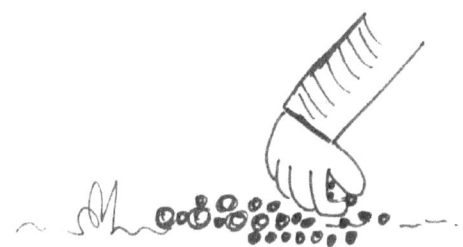

'And remember, I'm yer uncle,' Grimm snapped, as he unlocked and opened the coop door to let Benjamin out.

They arrived at the front door, where Grubb stood to one side and Miss Keys stood on the doorstep.

' 'Ere he is,' Grimm laughed nervously.

'Hello, Miss Keys,' said Benjamin quietly.

'Hello, Benjamin. Are you feeling OK?'

'Yes, much better now, thank you'.

'Have your uncles been looking after you today?'

Benjamin hesitated.

'Answer Miss Keys,' Grubb said, probably harsher than he'd intended. Grimm rested a hand firmly on the young boy's shoulder.

'What uncles?!' Benjamin yelled, and he turned around sharply, jumped up, and bit down hard onto Grimm's hand.

'Argghhh!!!' he screamed. 'Ya little runt!' Instinctively he let go of the boy's shoulder and clasped his hand. Benjamin made for the stairs close to where Grubb stood by the wall.

'No you don't!' Grubb cried, scuttling forwards towards Benjamin. But then he spotted Miss Keys reach for her bag and back away from the door.

'Get her!' Grubb boomed to Grimm.

Benjamin quickly changed direction and made for the kitchen. This caught Grubb unawares, but he regained his composure and set off in hot pursuit after the little runaway.

Chapter 14
Non-existent Gnashers

Benjamin ran down the hall and zipped into the kitchen. He was about to head out of the back door when suddenly the sizeable frame of Grievous filled it. He had heard Grimm's scream.

'What's happening?' he asked, puzzled.

'Catch that little runt!' Grubb yelled, still in pursuit.

Benjamin stopped just in front of Grievous, in fact right on Grievous' right foot. The nipper leaped up and, with both feet and all the force of a four-year-old, slammed down on it - HARD!

Grievous gave a yelp and reached out, but Benjamin was way too quick and leapt to the left, just as Grubb ran towards them. Grubb couldn't stop and slammed straight into Grievous. There was a colossal CRACKING noise as Grievous's glasses crunched on impact.

Grubb flew back with his legs flying high up into the air. Grievous just stood expressionless, peering through his cracked lenses, until he finally grimaced. As he did, all his visible teeth crumbled and spilled out of his mouth.

'Argghhh!!!' he screamed, reaching for his mouth, which was quickly becoming empty of any gnashers.

Benjamin smiled. He hurried across the kitchen and out of the other door which lead into the sitting room. Grubb stopped and took off his bonnet. He felt his billiard-ball head. It had indentations, like mice teeth marks in a stale chunk of cheese.

'You little swine!' he snapped, plonking his bonnet back on his noggin. He followed Benjamin into the sitting room.

The lad flew through the room and back into the hall. He looked behind him. Grimm had caught Miss Keys and was half carrying, half dragging her towards the kitchen. She was kicking and wriggling about madly. He stopped for one second. What could he do. He looked around - suddenly Grubb was right behind him.

'Leave him alone!' Miss Keys shouted. That was the last thing Benjamin heard as he charged up the stairs. Grubb dived for the boy's foot and caught it.

'Haha, got you now, you little parasite!'

But Benjamin quickly wriggled his foot out of Grubb's grasp.

'I don't think so, you big parasite!' Benjamin replied, as he reached the top of the stairs and dived right into his room. He closed the door behind him with a slam.

'Coming in, you little worm!'

Grubb turned the door handle. It wasn't even locked, how easy was this going to be! He stepped into the room and saw Benjamin. There he was at the window. The glass pane had been removed by Grimm, and the early evening breeze was blowing in. Benjamin was sitting right on the window ledge, with his feet dangling over the inside.

'You wouldn't be that stupid would you?' Grubb asked, stopping in the doorway. They were on the second floor, around ten metres up. The boy would at least break a bone if he jumped.

'See you!' Benjamin called, and he swung around and grabbed hold of the window sill on the outside.

'Come here!' Grubb yelled, moving forwards.

'Oh and one last thing ...' Benjamin called, peering up from outside the window '... mind your step!'

Grubb tried desperately to stop, but he was already committed. His right foot slid forwards. He tried to right himself with his left foot, but that slid too. Grubb looked at his feet which were now moving forwards and fast, like he was on skis. But he wasn't on skis. He was on a moving floor of hard rabbit droppings! When he looked up, he saw the window coming towards him. Grubb guessed he wouldn't be slowing down anytime soon, and you know what? He was right!

Chapter 15
Grubb goes to Ground

As Benjamin was slowly climbing down the stone exterior of the house, there was a yell from above. He watched as Grubb flew like a rocket out of his bedroom window. The yelling continued as the villain moved through the air with all the grace of a boulder, his arms flailing around him.

Benjamin closed his eyes as old Billiard Head landed on his back on the lawn with an almighty thud. Grubb was spreadeagled as if making a snow angel, and he was groaning like a wounded animal. Benjamin reached the ground and made for the hutch, where his dad and Miss Keys were now locked in. Time to get them out! But there was a problem. And that problem was round, and in urgent need of an optician and a dentist. And he was right in front of Benjamin.

'I don't fink so!' Grievous slurred, bits of tooth spitting out with every word. He reached forwards to grab Benjamin, but Grievous was now virtually blind, and was actually reaching out to a small bush.

'Benjamin!' Jeffrey and Miss Keys called together. 'Look out!'

'It's OK, I can see him,' Benjamin thought, 'which is more than can be said for him. He can't see anything.'

But when Benjamin looked

around, he realised they actually meant look out for the two others, who were swiftly closing in from behind him. Grubb was limping like a lame horse, but he had the face of a prowling lion, a lion which hadn't eaten for a month. Grimm just looked his normal horrible self. Benjamin couldn't help but notice the large nets that Grubb and Grimm were carrying. Maybe the ones they had used earlier to catch all those bats.

'Come here you little rat!' Grubb shouted, his eyes flickering like fire as he edged slowly forwards.

Benjamin glanced around for a split second, assessing his options. He had Grubb and Grimm behind him, and Grievous up ahead. His best option was forwards for sure. Grievous was the weak link.

Grubb must've sensed what Benjamin was thinking. 'Grievous, that's a bush you twit. The boy's here!' Grievous stopped grappling with the shrubbery, composed himself and brushed himself down.

'Sorry, Grubb. Just my glasses aren't any good no more.'

'They weren't any good in the first place!' Grubb snapped back. 'Just catch the little blob that moves!'

The three had Benjamin surrounded good and proper.

'Give yourself up, Benjamin. Let them do

what they want with the garden. As long as we're safe!' Jeffrey cried across.

'Yes, Benjamin, do what your dad says. You'll be safer in here!' Miss Keys added.

But Benjamin wasn't in any mood to give himself up, although he could've really done with a friend right now.

Chapter 16
Grot runs Riot

Benjamin looked straight ahead.

'No you don't,' Grievous sneered, his eyes flickering through the smashed glass of his specs. He crouched low with his arms outstretched and edged forwards, making Benjamin feel trapped. Benjamin looked behind him to the right.

'Don't even think about it!' Grimm snapped, flapping the huge net in front of him.

Then Benjamin looked behind him to the left.

'I don't think so, Benjamin. The game's up!' Grubb laughed, holding the net in front.

The scene looked like gamekeepers trying to catch an injured baby rhino in the African savannah.

'Go, get him, boy!' Grubb yelled, turning around.

Benjamin watched as Grot charged out of his kennel. He was fuming. There was steam come out of his nostrils. He darted straight for the young lad. The snarling was getting closer and closer.

'No!' Jeffrey screamed. They had a front row seat for this, even though they hadn't bought the ticket, or wanted a ticket for that matter.

Just then there was a flash of black and white between Grot and Benjamin. Grot's attention immediately swung to the pied flash. It came back and darted about in the air in front of Grot's nose. It gave a call. Benjamin and

Jeffrey immediately recognised the noise - it was the Major!

Grubb, Grimm and Grievous were all distracted, desperately trying to keep their sights on Benjamin. But the Major had a plan; he flew to the left towards Grubb, and Grot charged after him.

'No, no, not over here!' Grubb yelled, as the woodpecker flew low through Grubb's legs. Grot tried to do the same, but he was way too big and Grubb way too small. Instead he smashed straight into Grubb, who travelled backwards, clinging to Grot's substantial head.

'Stop, you great brute!'

But that was the last thing on Grot's mind. He kept on after the Major, who went straight for Grievous, next in line. Again the swift-moving woodpecker flew low, straight through Grievous's legs and then Grimm's, each time with Grot smacking into the men, and the men gripping onto Grot for dear life. Grubb first, then Grievous gripping Grubb and Grimm gripping Grievous, and all facing back to front.

Benjamin had space to escape; he charged forward. 'The hutch,' he thought.

'No, no, the Popular Poplar is where you want to go! Quickly into my home, please don't be too slow,' the Major shrieked over, apparently reading his mind.

Grot was in hot pursuit. Benjamin watched his woodpecker pal zigzag around the garden, keeping the stupid dog occupied as he made for the massive tree.

'Reach up and grab the trunk so high, then pull yourself up to the branch in the sky,' the Major shouted.

Benjamin reached the bottom of the Popular Poplar. He stretched his hands out and gripped onto the bark, and with his eyes closed, and all the force he could muster, pulled himself onto the first branch, and then the next one, and then the next. He scaled a tougher bit of the trunk where there were no branches, then reached the Major's home. Right on cue the woodpecker landed on the branch outside.

'Well done, little Ben, your dad will be proud, and up here we're safer away from that crowd!' his feathered friend said, wiping a wing over his brow.

'You're telling me!' Benjamin replied, blowing out.

Jeffrey had watched with astonishment as his young son scaled the tree, with what appeared to be help from the Major.

'That was amazing,' Rachel said. Jeffrey could only nod.

'RIGHT, THAT DOES IT!' came a voice from the foot of the poplar. It was Grubb, gingerly stepping off Grot. 'Stupid mutt!' he shouted, smacking Grot across the muzzle. It growled. 'GRIEVOUS!' he nodded to the toothless monster behind him. 'It's time to bring that big lump down!'

Chapter 17
Mr Grin's Final Performance is Rained off

The light was fading fast, and Grubb looked up at Benjamin, sitting high up on the poplar branch.

'We'll give you one last chance to come down, and one chance only!' Grubb barked. 'I'll count to three... ONE...TWO...'

Meanwhile, high in the poplar, Benjamin sat with the Major, both staring down.

Benjamin looked across at the woodpecker, who just raised his wing, as if to say, 'Wait'.

'THREE!' Grubb cried from below. 'OK, that's it! Grievous, your axe!' he boomed, turning to the toothless wonder.

'Wait, Grubb. I've got an idea to get the little sod down,' Grimm interjected, holding up his arm. 'Wait here for a second!'

Grimm turned and disappeared into the house. Grubb stood, his face getting redder and redder with every minute that his fiendish friend was away. After five minutes, the backdoor opened, but instead of Grimm, out popped Mr Grin, with a squirrel puppet on one hand and a rabbit puppet on the other. He was almost fully kitted out, with blue hair, red lips, white face and dirty apron, just minus the clown shoes.

Grubb grinned. 'What a great idea,' he thought. 'Oh, look who it is, hello, Mr Grin!' he shouted, glancing up at Benjamin.

'Mr Grin?!' Benjamin shouted down, puzzled.

'Hello, everyone!' Mr Grin shouted in a very high pitched voice, moving the rabbit puppet frantically.

'Benjamin! Benjamin! Wherefore art thou, Benjamin?' the squirrel puppet called.

'I'm up here. Staying away from those bad men,' Benjamin called down, pointing at Grubb and Grievous. 'And that bad dog!' he added.

'It's OK, my boy, you don't have to be afraid. Mr Grin is here now, and so are his friends Randolph the Rabbit and Sciurus the Squirrel!' he shouted back up, putting on the high pitched voices for each puppet in turn.

Jeremy and Rachel watched from the hutch as Benjamin nervously shuffled in the tree. They were actually hoping that Benjamin would be enticed down by Mr Grin. At least he would be down from the tree, and get locked in the hutch safely with them.

'What about him and him?' Benjamin called down, pointing to Grubb and then Grievous.

'They're not going to harm you,' said the rabbit. 'Are you guys?'

'Oh, of course not,' Grubb answered.

'We'll just be leaving,' Grievous added.

'You're going to leave?'

'Yes, we are,' Grubb said, winking at Mr Grin.

'And what about my dad and Miss Keys?'

'I'll let them out when you're down here. How does that sound?' Mr Grin answered.

Suddenly, it began to rain.

'OK, bye bye Mr Grubb, bye bye Mr Grievous,' the squirrel puppet called over in a silly voice. Both men turned around, and started to walk towards the house, Grubb peering over his shoulder to watch the reaction of the small boy in the tree.

'OK,' Benjamin said, looking at the Major. The woodpecker looked unsure. 'It's Mr Grin, he's nice,' Benjamin said. The Major looked inquisitively down at the clown far below.

'OK, Mr Grin!' Benjamin called. 'I'm coming down!'

Mr Grin looked up and smiled. 'Yeah come down Benjamin! We're all your friends down here!' he added, with the squirrel and then the rabbit puppet.

Suddenly, Mr Grin tasted something sweet in his mouth, and then something horrible and lumpy. 'What the…' he thought, rubbing his fingers on his lips. When he looked down his hand was purple and it had lots of horrible lumpy white flour in it. This meant only one thing; the rain had washed the blue dye from his hair into the red dye of his lips, and the flour from his face into his mouth. Mr Grin was looking more and more like Mr Grimm with every second. He had to act quickly.

'Come on, Benjamin. Chop, chop my little friend!' the squirrel puppet shouted up.

'Wait, young Ben...' the woodpecker spoke. 'That's not Mr Grin, it's that other bloke!'

'Grimm, yeah, one of the animal killers is he, if he gets his way, he'll chop my house down, and then have me for tea!'

Benjamin looked down at the man standing at the bottom of the poplar. Indeed, the blue spiky hair was now gone, as were the bright red lips and white face. It was Grimm. Mr Grimm was Mr Grin!

Benjamin stopped and pulled himself back up onto the branch.

'I'm not coming down. You're a baddy too!' Benjamin shouted down.

Grubb and Grievous had heard Benjamin and they walked back out into the garden.

'Good try, Grimm,' Grubb barked. 'But it's now time for more persuasive measures!'

Chapter 18
Battle-lines are Drawn

That night, Grievous and Grot sat guarding the tree, Grimm sat watching over Jeremy and Rachel in the hutch, and Grubb kept watch from inside the house (apparently). The poplar would be toppled in the morning. The date was set.

Meanwhile, the Major invited young Benjamin into his home for the night, which was a bit of a squeeze.

'Are you sure I can't interest you in a beetle juice, it's very a delightful treat; it gives you strength in your arms and wings, and a spring in your feet!' the woodpecker yelped, flapping his wings and springing up into the air.

'No, really, I'm good, thank you,' Benjamin replied, having to duck his head to fit in the hole. He was thirsty and hungry, but beetle juice, beetle stew, beetle tart or anything else with beetle in it didn't sound that appealing.

'So, what are we going to do, Major? They're going to chop the Popular Poplar down!'

'Calm down my child, I have just the idea, to stop these ghastly killers, without any fear,' the woodpecker said, and he took a slurp of his juice.

'What are we going to do?'

'The emphasis is on 'we' my young friend, we can't do this alone. Good evening everyone and welcome to my home!' the woodpecker called, raising a wing and looking towards the entrance. By moonlight, Benjamin watched as shadows of creatures appeared and all squeezed into the Major's home. Benjamin could hardly breath, he was getting so squashed.

'Do we have the bat battalion? Give me a call if you're here.'

'Yes, Sir, all present and correct, over here at the rear!' There was a series of winged waves from the back of the gathered crowd.

'Good, good. And how about the bird brigade, are you here too?'

'Yes, Sir, we are indeed; just tell us what to do!'

'Fabulous. And finally, the squirrel squadron, can you help defend us all from the horrors below?'

'Yes, Sir, you can count on us; we would never have said no!'

'Good, good,' the Major yelled with glee. 'Now, please gather round and make sure that you can see.'

'Here, my friends, I've drawn up some plans, to save our treasured home from the cruellest of clans!' The woodpecker removed a wooden picture frame on the wall of his home, and turned it over revealing a diagram of squiggles, lines and other symbols.

Everyone sat hunched forward, watching intently as the Major pointed to the plan and then threw his wings about frantically to show where each group should be.

By the time he had finished, everyone knew what had to be done.

Meanwhile, at the base of the poplar, Grot was getting restless and he sat growling up at the tree. He started to gnaw at the thick trunk and pull large chunks of bark off.

'Eashey boy,' Grievous called over through his broken gnashers. 'Shave it for tomorrow.'

Grot stopped, but he had one last message to give the poplar. He went back up to the base and lifted his back leg. 'Message received?' Grot questioned with a toothy grin.

Chapter 19
When Animals Attack!

The next morning, just before dawn, the peace and quiet was cut short by the scream of a grown man from inside Brockholes Manor. It was Grubb, and he didn't sound best pleased.

'ARGGHHH!' he screamed, bursting out of the back door and into the garden. Grimm, Grievous and Grot were dozing, but all had had about as little sleep as one another. They all turned around.

'Wot the...?' Grimm shouted.

'Bats! Bats! There's bats everywhere!' he screamed. And Grubb was right, bats were flooding out of the house, through the open windows and out of the back door, and Billiard Head had them on him, under his clothes, absolutely everywhere.

He quickly took off his jumper, exposing his vest, and knocked off the bats which were under it, then just as swiftly ripped his trousers off, showing off a pair of garish yellow-with-purple-polka-dots boxer shorts. There were bats all over them as well! He kept running,

knocking them away.

'The bats, they're out for revenge!' he screamed.

'Enough o' this,' Grimm called, grabbing a net and swiping at the cloud of bats flying about, with Grievous doing the same.

Suddenly, Grimm started to wriggle as well, and he began to laugh hysterically.

'Ha, no get off!' he cried out, chucking his net  down and thrashing his hands about his body. It was then that two squirrels appeared - one from under his shirt at the neck, and the other from his shirt sleeve.

'Why you little pests!' he screamed. Simultaneously, the squirrels bit down hard on Grimm - one on his hand, and the other on his ear.

'Argghhh! Not again?!' He belted the squirrels off, but more and more came and disappeared under his clothes, until he was doing a funky jig.

What a spectacle this was for Benjamin and the Major, who sat by the old woodpecker's hole looking down, and also for Jeffrey and Rachel who had front row seats for the best show in town. Grimm started to fling off his clothes as well, knocking off squirrel after squirrel.

'Get off me!'

Grievous tried to help Grimm and Grubb by swishing

his net madly at the bats and squirrels. He couldn't really see them, but he did manage to catch the odd one. The creatures were still coming at them thick and fast.

'INCOMING!' Grimm screamed, as he watched a swarm of birds fly towards Grievous.

'What?!' yelled Grievous, swinging around. He didn't have time to swoosh his net. They were on him and they were pecking at him.

'Get off, you!' he shouted. Then another wave of birds arrived, and dropped their white watery loads all over him.

'ARGGHHH!' he bellowed, the last of his crumbled teeth spraying from his mouth like crunched up mints.

He, too, started to whip off his shirt and trousers, both thick with bird poo. He was soon reduced to his boxer shorts and vest.

'Dishgushting!' he yelled, as the birds continued to shed their loads, while others pecked him like a suet ball on a bird table.

'Now, it's my turn to do my bit, that mutt Grot is in for a hit!' the Major said, turning to Benjamin and winking.

The woodpecker took off and headed straight to Grot, who was looking around without a clue where to go and which critters to chase.

'I'll make it easy for him,' the woodpecker thought.

Benjamin watched as his pal flew at the face of the brute and started to peck wildly at his huge head. Grot tried to swot the black and white bird away, but the Major was way too quick. Next he flew up and round in mini circles right in front of Grot. The beast was angry, and he was only after one thing now. The Major shot to the right with Grot in hot pursuit.

Benjamin watched from above at the scene which wouldn't have been out of place in a circus. All three men were stripped to their glaring boxer shorts and vests, and were wildly swatting at the squirrels, bats and birds which were tearing around them, while Grot was charging around after the Major like a deranged bull.

But then things took a turn for the worse.

Chapter 20
It Hits the Back of the Net!

The Major glanced back, and Grot was still coming after him. That was good. What wasn't so good was what was happening elsewhere. The tide was turning, it seemed. The terrible trio were now on the offensive. Large numbers of animals were now caught in the dreaded nets with only a few squirrels, bats and birds still putting up a fight.

As the woodpecker turned around to see Grot, he took his eye from the front where Grimm's nasty net loomed. The pied bird shot straight into the net like a David Beckham free kick.

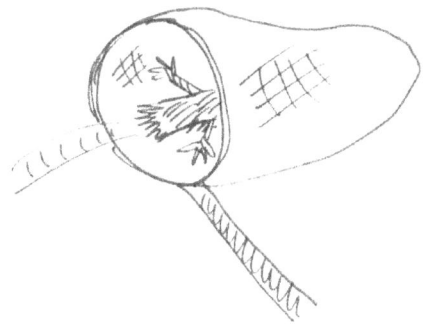

'Ha!' Grimm laughed. 'We've got 'im!'

Jeffrey and Rachel looked at each other in distress, and then up to Benjamin who they could see still on the poplar branch.

'OK, let's finish this once and for all!' Grubb screamed, trapping the last of the creatures in the net. 'Grievous, bring three axes. This shouldn't take too long!'

Chapter 21
Growing Pains

'No!' Jeffrey screamed, grabbing the hutch door with both hands and rattling it. He watched as the intruders grabbed an axe each and stood by the base of the poplar. The nets were left on the ground, with their entrances folded over, so the animals were trapped inside.

'Right, boys, let's bring her down!' Grubb cried, swinging the axe back.

'Benjamin!' The Major screamed from inside the net. 'Get into my house, and hurry, it's your safest bet! The poplar will protect you from these retched crooks, but you must hurry quickly, as you don't have long, by the looks!'

Sure enough, Benjamin could see Grubb, Grimm, Grievous and Grot start to attack the base of the tremendous tree trunk. Bits of tree bark flew off in all directions as the three axes crashed into the trunk, whilst the dog ravaged the tree with his muzzle, stripping and spitting pieces everywhere.

'We've got to do something!' Jeffrey cried, looking at Rachel and rattling the hutch door again. But it was no good. The door wasn't going anywhere and either were they.

After the best part of an hour, around half of the trunk of the poplar had been violently severed off. In the cavity high up in the trunk, Benjamin could hear the great tree creaking and groaning. Was it in pain, he thought? The others heard the sound too.

'What's that noise?' Grubb asked, looking around at Grievous.

'Oh, that? Trees often make that noische when they're schtraining, eschpecially the big 'unsch.'

'Sounds like it's groanin' to me,' Grimm said.

'Don't be stupid,' Grubb snapped. 'Trees don't groan!' But this one did.

Chapter 22
The Last Stand

Another series of chop, chop, chops from the axes and gnaw, gnaw and gnaws from Grot, and the poplar was starting to sway. The noise it was making was now almost unbearable.

'That's groanin' that is!' Grimm shouted.

'Shut up!' Grubb snapped.

The Major had a tear in his eye, as did many of the other animals with him in the nets.

'Our home!' cried a bat.

'It's going to fall!' yelled a dove.

'It can't fall down. It's all we've got, our great home high above!'

But the massive tree was going to fall down.

'Grievous, we want it down over that way!' Grubb yelled over the straining noise from the poplar, pointing away from the house.

'What way?' the visually challenged forester asked, looking in the opposite direction from Grubb. 'Away-from-the-house way, you buffoon!'

'Oh yeah, sure fing! If we cut a triangle here, we'll be able to pusch it in that directschon.'

With that, Grievous chopped at one side of the massive trunk; the poplar now tilted to one side.

'Ready, juscht needs a few more chopsch, get

right back!' Chop, chop, chop, sway, swAAAYYY, SWAAAAYYYY. The poplar started its descent.

'It's coming!' Grubb yelled, with delight.

Benjamin held on for dear life. He closed his eyes and hoped for the best, but feared the worst.

Chapter 23
The Bigger they are, the Harder they Fall

The poplar was falling, and it was falling exactly where Grievous intended it to - a textbook tree fell.

However, all of a sudden the earth violently broke underneath the huge poplar as if an earthquake had been triggered, and roots started to tear up through the ground like tentacles of a great sea monster. Benjamin felt the poplar judder and stall, before it appeared to pivot on its huge roots, most which were now exposed above the ground, and start to fall in the opposite direction - very much not a textbook tree fell.

'What on earth—' Grievous called, the axe falling from his hands.

Suddenly a huge root from the poplar shot out of the ground and catapulted the bespectacled baddy skywards. He flew through the air like a rocket and disappeared from sight. There was a dull thud in the distance.

Grubb gulped. 'Run!'

Grot charged into his kennel, Grubb ran off to the left, and Grimm to the right. The poplar flew through the air and downwards. Some of the branches snapped off. Jeffrey and Rachel held their breath as the tree continued to fall. The first large branch crashed to the ground before it ricocheted violently and landed right

on top of Grot's kennel, which instantly crumbled under the weight.

Grubb called out. 'Grot!' He stopped and looked up at the poplar. Much to his horror, the main trunk had changed direction again, and was now coming right for him. He had no time. First a piece of splintered branch crashed down onto his feet.

'ARGGHHH!!!' But his shouting was cut short as the trunk crashed down on him.

Grimm heard the shout and spun around. He had got away from the tree, but the others weren't so lucky. He watched as the rest of the main tree crashed to the ground. A pleasant thought then came to his mind. With a sly smile he realised he wouldn't have to split the profits made from the poplar timber by three. He was going to be even richer! But that thought was short-lived, as was Grimm, who forgot to look up!

Chapter 24
On Solid Ground

Another splintering branch had broken away and smashed straight down onto Grimm. Jeffrey and Rachel watched as he was swallowed up by the ground under the weight of the branch.

'Look out!' Jeffrey shouted, pulling Rachel to the ground as another huge branch crashed down right onto the front of the hutch, the door instantly rupturing under the impact.

'Come on, let's get out of here!' Jeffrey shouted, helping Rachel out of the broken door.

'Benjamin!' he called, when they were both safely out and running across to the Major's hole. 'Benjamin! Benjamin! Are you alright?'

When he got to the entrance of the hole he peered in, and, sure enough, his son was still in there, but he looked motionless.

'Benjamin, are you OK?' Jeffrey asked, reaching forwards to grab his still boy.

Benjamin opened his eyes groggily and murmured, 'Dad, has the tree stopped falling yet?'

Chapter 25
Down But Not Out

Jeffrey helped his son out of the woodpecker hole and gave him the longest hug ever.

'Thank God you're safe.'

'You gave us quite a scare,' Rachel smiled, giving Benjamin a hug as well.

'Where'd you learn to climb like that, by the way?' Jeffrey asked.

'You're a good teacher,' Benjamin replied, 'and so is the Major.'

Jeffrey smiled at Benjamin, and then at Rachel.

'The Major! Over here!'

Benjamin quickly led the three of them across to the bulging nets and picked them up. The animals - bats, birds and squirrels - solemnly clambered out of the nets, every one of them quietly saying thank you to Benjamin as they escaped. They all moved across and stood on the stricken poplar tree. It was then that Jeffrey noticed a grimy bandana on the ground beside a large branch.

'Grimm's?' Jeffrey asked no-one in particular.

'Mr Grin's,' Rachel added.

Together they lifted the branch up a little and looked under it. There was a large hole in the ground, like an open manhole, and it looked like it went on and on forever, deep into the core of the earth. It was just a black hole, no sign of the former pie-maker and children's entertainer. He was gone, and gone for GOOD.

They continued to walk around the poplar in silence. The animals sat with their heads bowed, scattered along the tree. Next, Jeffrey noticed a brown, worn out bonnet by the side of the tremendous trunk.

'Grubb's?' he said, picking it up and dusting it down. It was still dirty. Again, underneath the trunk was an open hole where the fallen tree had knocked the squat scoundrel into the pit of doom.

Finally, down at what was the root end of the tree, lay a filthy green cap which read 'Hefty Grievous'. This had obviously flown off his head when he was knocked into next week.

Jeffrey walked across to the main trunk of the poplar and sat down on one of the branches. He rested his hand on its gnarly bark. This tree meant everything to him, and to Benjamin, and to everyone else. He looked

around at the Major and all the animals sitting perched on its huge bulk, in silence.

Jeffrey felt tears well up, just as Rachel sat down next to him and gripped his hand. Benjamin came across and sat down next to his father too. Jeffrey smiled at Rachel, and put an arm around his son. They all looked around, where the poplar giant was now sprawled out as if sleeping, its large branches scattered across the garden. Even though the Popular Poplar had been toppled, its leaves still gently swayed in the light morning breeze, making a gentle crinkling noise.

Jeffrey looked down at Benjamin and then at Rachel, who was still holding his hand, and it was then that he realised everything would be alright.

Epilogue

Two years later, Miss Keys became Mrs Bumpkin, as Jeffrey and Rachel married at the same church that you could now see from the kitchen window of their home, Brockholes Manor. And, speaking of Brockholes Manor, it was now fully furnished with the nicest wooden furniture that you've ever seen. Stunning, striking and strong black poplar wood. The house now also had a loft space which was home to all the animals which had once lived in the Popular Poplar. And the Major – well, he had a luxurious bird box (made from poplar wood of course) on the side of the manor house all to himself!

All the residents of Brockholes Manor were happy once again, and there was nothing that the new Bumpkin family enjoyed more than sitting in the garden and watching the sun setting above the young black poplar saplings swaying in the breeze where the Popular Poplar once stood. Perhaps one day they would be as prominent and popular as the Popular Poplar once was.

THE END

Dr Colin Bonnington

Colin works as an ecological consultant based in Manchester. He writes and illustrates wildlife themed stories based on his experiences during his work. He completed a doctorate at the University of Sheffield on the impact of grey squirrels on birds, and still regularly writes scientific journal articles. *Benjamin Bumpkin and the Treasured Tree* is his third book for children. Colin lives in Cheshire with his cat and his wife (and at the moment, her baby bump!).

www.ingramcontent.com/pod-product-compliance
Lightning Source LLC
Chambersburg PA
CBHW050041080526
44586CB00014B/1401